WHAT DO YOU KNOW ABOUT

Relationships

PETE SANDERS and STEVE MYERS

COPPER BEECH BOOKS

BROOKFIELD, CONNECTICUT

Designed and produced by
Aladdin Books Ltd
28 Percy Street
London W1P 0LD

First published
in the United States in 1998 by
Copper Beech Books,
an imprint of
The Millbrook Press
2 Old New Milford Road
Brookfield, Connecticut 06804

Printed in Belgium

Design   David West
                Children's
                Book Design
Editor   Jen Green
Picture research Brooks-
                Krikler
                Research
Illustrator   Mike Lacy

Library of Congress
Cataloging-in-Publication Data
Sanders. Pete.
Relationships / Pete Sanders and Steve Myers ;
illustrated by Mike Lacey.
p. cm. — (What do you know about)
Summary: Examines different kinds of
relationships in the areas of friendship,
families, and love, discussing why they work
and what to do when they do not work.
ISBN 0-7613-0873-3 (lib. bdg.)
1. Interpersonal relations in children—Juvenile
literature. 2. Interpersonal relations—Juvenile
literature. [1. Interpersonal relations.]
I. Myers, Steve. II. Lacey, Mike, ill.
III. Title. IV. Series: Sanders, Pete.
What do you know about.
BF723.I646S26   1998 98-16971
158.2—dc21   CIP AC

CONTENTS

HOW TO USE THIS BOOK
The books in this series are intended to help young people to understand more about issues that may affect their lives. Each book can be read by a child, or together with a parent, teacher, or guardian so that there is an opportunity to talk through ideas as they come up. The questions that appear on the storyline pages throughout the book are intended to invite further discussion.

At the end of the book there is a section called "What Can We Do?" This section provides practical ideas that will be useful for both young people and adults, as well as a list of names and addresses for further information and support.

INTRODUCTION

THROUGHOUT OUR LIVES WE COME INTO CONTACT WITH MANY PEOPLE. THE RELATIONSHIPS WE FORM WITH OTHERS ARE VERY IMPORTANT.

Relationships make a great difference in the quality of our lives. Communication with other people can help us to feel valued, supported, and cared for.

This book will help you to understand more about the different kinds of relationships there are, and how they can affect you. Each chapter introduces a different aspect of the subject, illustrated by a continuing storyline. The characters in the story have to deal with situations that many of us will experience ourselves. After each episode we stop and look at the issues raised, and broaden the discussion. By the end, you should know more about the importance of relationships, how they can make you feel and act, and the effect they can have on your life.

I'M SORRY I WAS HORRIBLE TO ARCHIE. HE'S REALLY NICE. BUT IT'S NOT THE SAME.

RELATIONSHIPS TAKE TIME, GARY. SOMETIMES PEOPLE TRY TOO HARD. YOU HAVE TO BE CERTAIN OF YOUR OWN FEELINGS.

DIFFERENT KINDS OF RELATIONSHIPS

A RELATIONSHIP IS THE BOND OR CONNECTION BETWEEN TWO PEOPLE. IT IS BUILT ON THE WAY THOSE PEOPLE THINK AND FEEL ABOUT ONE ANOTHER.

There are two different types of relationships: Those we can choose and those we have no choice about. For example, we choose our friends, but have no choice about who is in our family.

There are many possible levels of relationship. Some people we feel very strongly about, others we do not. We might have many friends, but only one or two we are close to. Adults may have a special person they choose to share their lives with.

We don't relate to everyone in the same way. The way you talk to other young people might be very different from the way you talk to a teacher or another adult. Certain relationships are very casual or last only a short time. Others may last our whole lives. Each may mean a great deal to us.

We can enjoy different kinds of relationships at the same time.

▽ Gary Hopkins had just moved into the neighborhood with his mom, Brenda, and sister, Julie.

THAT MUST BE THE NEW KID. LOOK AT THE WAY HE'S DRESSED.

YOU'LL BE ALRIGHT GARY. YOU'RE BOUND TO FEEL NERVOUS WHEN YOU DON'T KNOW ANYONE.

THIS IS GARY. HE'S JUST MOVED HERE FROM THE SOUTH. I WANT YOU TO MAKE HIM FEEL WELCOME.

I BET HE TALKS FUNNY.

SHHH! HE'LL HEAR YOU.

▽ Every lunchtime, Richard and Rob played soccer with their friends. The gang was nicknamed "the Adventurers."

WE HAVE EVEN NUMBERS. YOU'LL HAVE TO FIND SOMEONE ELSE TO PLAY WITH.

▽ That evening, Gary's sister, Julie, told him about her first day at her new school.

MR. ANDERSON, MY GYM TEACHER, IS GORGEOUS. EVERYONE WAS REALLY FRIENDLY.

▽ Julie made a face at Gary and left the room, laughing.

I NEVER WANTED TO COME HERE IN THE FIRST PLACE.

△ Gary felt miserable. He was missing his old friends and hated the way the gang was treating him.

NOW DON'T RUB IT IN, JULIE. YOU KNOW GARY'S HAD A ROUGH DAY.

YOU KNOW WE HAD TO. GIVE IT A CHANCE. THINGS WILL GET BETTER SOON, I PROMISE.

Gary misses his friends from his old school, and is feeling lonely.

There is nothing wrong with being alone: Most of us like to be on our own at some time. Loneliness is very different. Friends often influence the way we feel about ourselves. Thinking that nobody wants to know you, or cares about you, can make you lose some of your self-respect, and this may be very difficult to deal with.

Gary and Julie have started at new schools. Gary is feeling left out and miserable.

Being the newcomer in a situation is not always easy. Sometimes being nervous can prevent you from acting naturally. Some people, like Julie, find it easy to make new friends. Others may find it harder to mix with people they don't know, particularly if they are shy. It can take longer for people to get to know and accept you, especially if you are thought to be different in some way.

The Adventurers are Rob and Richard's gang and they like to play together a lot.

There is nothing wrong with being part of a group of friends who have a really good time together. Sometimes, though, the people in a gang are not true friends. They may be rivals, and dare each other to do things. In a gang situation it can often be hard to refuse to do what the others are doing, even if you know it is wrong. This can lead to trouble.

FRIENDSHIP

FRIENDSHIP IS ONE OF THE MOST IMPORTANT KINDS OF RELATIONSHIPS, BECAUSE WE EACH DECIDE FOR OURSELVES WHO OUR FRIENDS ARE.

We tend to use the word "friend" to mean everyone we know and like. But friends are not just people you know well. They are people you care about and who care about you.

Some people have lots of friends – others choose to have only a few. You may see different friends for different purposes. You may have one friend you like to go out and do things with; you may have another with whom you like to discuss your feelings, because you value their opinion. Close friends might reveal things about themselves to each other that they would not tell anyone else.

A true friend is a person you can rely on. Those who say things like "If you won't do this, I won't be your friend anymore" are not real friends in the first place, because they are trying to force you into doing something you don't want to do. They are using their power to stop being your "friend" as a threat.

Some friends may not see each other very often, but remain good friends even so.

▽ It was the end of Gary's third day at his new school.

HI, GARY. I LOVE COMPUTER GAMES- CAN I TAKE A LOOK?

OF COURSE.

MY MOM AND DAD HAVE SPLIT UP, SO WE'VE COME TO STAY WITH MY GRANDPARENTS. I ONLY SEE MY DAD EVERY OTHER WEEKEND.

◁ Rob asked why Gary had moved to the area.

▽ Rob said his mom had just remarried.

IT'S HARD WHEN YOUR DAD'S NOT AROUND, ISN'T IT? MINE DIED FIVE YEARS AGO.

WOULD YOU LIKE TO COME TO MY HOUSE? I HAVE LOTS OF OTHER COMPUTER GAMES.

I'D LOVE TO, BUT I CAN'T. I'M WAITING FOR RICHARD. WE'RE GOING TO THE BOY'S CLUB.

◁ Gary and Rob said goodbye, and Rob set off with Richard to meet the rest of the gang.

▽ Rob suddenly realized that Richard was very moody, and asked him what was wrong.

WHAT WERE YOU TALKING TO HIM FOR?

GARY SEEMS REALLY NICE. I THINK YOU'RE JUST JEALOUS OF HIM.

HE'S JUST TRYING TO BUY FRIENDS WITH HIS COMPUTER GAMES. YOU CAN'T BE FRIENDS WITH HIM AND PART OF THE GANG, TOO.

Do you think Richard is right?

Rob and Richard are best friends. A best friend is someone you can share everything with, both good and bad.
Many people have a particular friend that they feel closer to than others. This will be a relationship built on trust and a genuine concern for each other's feelings. It is possible, though, to have a special friendship with one person and still enjoy being friends with others too. Richard is afraid that Gary will be a threat to his relationship with Rob. But if the friendship is really strong, this need not be a problem.

Finding you have something in common with another person is often the first step to becoming friends.
Rob and Gary have found they both like to play computer games and have similar family backgrounds. Making friends can also be easier if you are able to talk to a person alone, without other people around who might affect the way you or the other person behave.

Richard was wrong about Gary. Sometimes, however, people do try to "buy" friendship.
This can also work the other way around. A person may pretend to be a friend to get access to something someone else owns. It is not always easy to spot a person's motives. People who claim to like you because they want to get something out of you are not true friends.

FAMILIES

JUST AS THERE ARE SEVERAL KINDS OF RELATIONSHIPS, THERE ARE ALSO MANY DIFFERENT KINDS OF FAMILIES.

To most people, family means a group of people related by blood or marriage. But not everyone's family situation is the same. Some families are very large, others quite small. Not all families have both a mother and a father. Not all parents are married. Some children are orphans, or have been adopted, or live as part of a stepfamily. The love between young people and adults in these families can be just as strong as in other families.

People usually expect families to be close. However, families can experience the same kind of problems as other relationships. We do not choose our family, and might not have picked certain members of our family as friends. It can sometimes take a lot of effort on everyone's part to get along together.

Some children live with just one of their parents — perhaps because one parent has died, or because they have divorced or separated.

▽ Two weeks later, Gary and Rob had become friends. Rob invited Gary back to his house after school.

MOM SAYS IT'S OKAY, AS LONG AS I AM BACK BY 6 O'CLOCK.

ARE YOU SURE A RUN WOULDN'T DO YOU MORE GOOD THAN THOSE GAMES?

DON'T PAY ATTENTION TO HIM, GARY. HE'S JUST WANTS US OUT OF THE WAY SO HE CAN PLAY WITH THEM HIMSELF.

△ For the first time in a long time, Gary felt happy, listening to Rob and his stepdad joking.

▷ Rob told Gary that his stepdad used to try too hard to be friends with him.

YOUR STEPDAD'S REALLY FUN.

YES, HE IS. IT TOOK A WHILE TO GET TO KNOW EACH OTHER. I DIDN'T WANT TO LIKE HIM AT FIRST.

I DON'T THINK I GAVE HIM AN EASY TIME.

I THINK I'D DO THE SAME. I REALLY MISS MY DAD. I COULDN'T BEAR THE THOUGHT OF ANYONE TAKING HIS PLACE.

SHE'S REALLY MAD. I'D BETTER GET A MOVE ON.

OK. I'LL SEE YOU TOMORROW.

△ Gary realized they had lost track of time. It was seven o'clock.

▷ Gary rushed home, wondering what his mom would say.

△ Gary and Julie began to argue.

△ Grandpa had been ill for months, and stayed in bed.

What are Gary and Julie really arguing about?

Gary and Julie often argue. Living with brothers and sisters can be trying at times.
If it seems one brother or sister is getting away with something, or being treated differently, this can feel unfair. Sometimes a difference in age can lead to problems. The relationship between brothers and sisters often changes as they grow older. Strangely enough, though they may fight amongst themselves, they will sometimes be the first to stick up for each other when necessary.

Gary was late getting home and his mom was angry.
Parents often lay down certain rules that they expect you to follow. They may tell you to be home by a particular time, or have strong views about what you can and cannot watch on television. You may feel that you should not have to be told what to do. But most parents impose these rules because they care about you. As you get older, they will allow you more freedom to make your own decisions.

Gary and Julie's grandpa is ill. Their mother is glad to help out.
Most of us rely on our parents to take care of us when we are young. In later life, our parents may need our help to look after them. We may have to give them the same care and attention as they gave us as children.

Stepfamilies can face problems of their own.
When Rob's father died, he and his mom became a family on their own. When his mom remarried, it took a long time for Rob to grow to like and trust his new stepfather. It can be painful to accept new people into a family, especially if you think it will change the relationships between other family members.

ATTRACTION

NOBODY CAN SAY FOR CERTAIN WHAT ATTRACTS ONE PERSON TO ANOTHER.

It might be the way that person looks or speaks, or how we feel when he or she is near. Sometimes we may not fully understand ourselves why we find that particular person attractive.

You might find someone's personality attractive. Perhaps they are very sociable and outgoing – always cracking jokes and making you laugh. Or you might be attracted to somebody who is quiet and reserved.

The way someone looks is often the first thing we notice. It is not a good idea, though, to judge a person only by physical appearance. First impressions can't always be trusted. Sometimes you decide right away that you like someone. But it can take time for attraction to happen.

You will also feel different kinds of attraction. You might like someone and want to be their friend. Or you might feel emotionally or sexually attracted to another person, particularly as you get older. The first feelings of sexual attraction can be difficult to cope with, especially if you are unable to talk to anyone else about them.

Not everyone is attracted by the same kinds of people. Attraction happens for all types of reasons.

▽ Weeks later, Gary, Julie, and Brenda were shopping.

HEY, THERE'S ROB AND HIS MOM. LET'S GO OVER.

▷ Rob and Gary had been friends for three months now, but their families had never met.

▽ Julie was worried about missing Pete Alexander.

WHY DON'T WE GO FOR COFFEE?

OK. JULIE WANTS TO BE AT THE BOOKSTORE IN HALF AN HOUR. PETE ALEXANDER IS SIGNING COPIES OF HIS BOOK.

I NEVER MISS HIS T.V. SHOW. I THINK HE'S REALLY COOL.

HE'S NOT DUE TO ARRIVE UNTIL 2 O'CLOCK.

IT'S A CRUSH. SHE WAS LIKE THIS LAST OCTOBER WITH HER NEW TEACHER.

I LIKE JULIE—SHE'S REALLY A LOT OF FUN.

WHY DON'T YOU TWO STAY HERE? WE'LL TAKE JULIE TO THE BOOKSTORE, WON'T WE GARY?

I SUPPOSE SO.

YOU DON'T HAVE TO PUT UP WITH HER ALL THE TIME.

△ Gary couldn't understand why Rob was acting like this.

▷ Meanwhile Brenda and Rob's mom, Joan, were having a good chat.

I'VE NEVER SEEN ROB LIKE THAT BEFORE. I THINK HE'S TAKEN A LIKING TO JULIE.

THAT'S ALL I NEED. I HAVE ENOUGH PROBLEMS AS IT IS.

▽ Brenda told Joan about Archie, someone she had met at work.

JUST BE HONEST WITH THEM. IT'S NEVER EASY WHEN YOU MEET SOMEBODY NEW.

▽ Gary soon returned.

WHERE ARE THE OTHER TWO?

HE ASKED ME TO GO OUT WITH HIM. I DREAD TO THINK HOW GARY AND JULIE WILL TAKE IT.

ROB SAID HE WANTED TO ASK JULIE SOMETHING PRIVATE. THEY'LL BE KISSING AND CUDDLING SOON.

YOU'VE NEVER COMPLAINED ABOUT MY HUGS.

STOP IT MOM. THAT WAS OKAY WHEN I WAS LITTLE. THIS IS GIRL'S STUFF.

WHY DO BOYS THINK IT'S ONLY GIRLS WHO CAN SHOW AFFECTION? I DON'T UNDERSTAND IT.

ROB'S JUST THE SAME. HE'LL LET ME HUG HIM IF WE'RE ALONE. BUT IF HIS FRIENDS ARE THERE, I HAVE NO CHANCE.

I THINK YOU'LL LIKE THE YOUTH CLUB. THEY PLAY SOME GREAT MUSIC ON SATURDAY NIGHT. WILL YOU GO WITH ME?

IF MOM SAYS IT'S ALRIGHT.

Do you agree cuddling is "girl's stuff?"

Julie has a "crush" on Pete Alexander.
A crush is a strong set of emotions that makes you feel attracted to somebody, even though you know very little about them. It might be a teacher, someone on T.V. or in movies, a pop star – or just someone you know casually. Sometimes people have a crush on a person of the same sex. Crushes tend to last only a short while. They can be confusing, but are perfectly natural.

The way people are shown in movies, on T.V., and in newspapers can affect the way we feel about them.
Julie thinks Pete Alexander is "sexy," and believes she knows what he is like. However, she only knows what she has seen on T.V. or read in magazines. She is attracted to the image Pete Alexander is choosing to present. In reality, he may be very different from how he appears to be.

Gary was embarrassed because his mom tried to cuddle him.
It may seem strange that in our society males and females are expected to act in different ways. You may have been told that boys aren't supposed to cry, or that girls shouldn't act tough. Other societies and cultures have ideas and customs that are very different. Emotions affect all of us, and showing affection is a natural human response. It is important for everyone to be able to do this, not just women and girls.

INTIMATE RELATIONSHIPS

AT SOME POINT IN LIFE, MOST OF US WILL MEET SOMEBODY TO WHOM WE ARE PARTICULARLY ATTRACTED.

We may decide this is the person with whom we want to spend the majority of our time, and perhaps share the rest of our life.
Some men and women decide to get married. Others choose to live together without marrying. Some adults choose to live with a partner of the same sex. In some cultures, parents decide who their children will marry. No matter what the situation, the commitment to the relationship can be equally as strong.

Making this commitment is an important decision. Many people think that it should not be made until we are old enough to understand ourselves and others well. Sometimes, people want to form a close relationship because they think it is the way they ought to behave. They may feel that others will see them as peculiar if they do not have someone who is "special." Having a boyfriend or girlfriend just to impress others is not a good idea.

Intimate relationships can be enjoyed by adults of all ages.

▽ The following Saturday, Rob took Julie out.

YOU'RE REALLY FUN TO BE WITH, JULIE.

THANKS. THIS IS A GREAT PLACE.

▷ Gary spent his Saturday evening watching T.V. with his grandma. At nine o'clock his mom came home with a visitor.

MOM, GARY— I'D LIKE YOU TO MEET A FRIEND OF MINE. THIS IS ARCHIE.

PLEASED TO MEET YOU.

▽ Everyone seemed very nervous. There wasn't much conversation.

I NEED TO PICK UP JULIE FROM THE YOUTH CLUB.

I'D BE HAPPY TO DRIVE YOU.

▽ Brenda and Archie left. Gary was upset. He told his grandma how much he still missed his dad.

▽ Gary always found his grandma easy to talk to. He told her how he was feeling.

DON'T YOU WORRY I'M JUST WONDERING WHAT YOUR GRANDPA'S GOING TO HAVE TO SAY ABOUT ARCHIE.

I DON'T SUPPOSE MOM WILL HAVE MUCH TIME FOR ME ANYMORE. NEITHER WILL ROB NOW THAT HE'S SEEING JULIE.

OF COURSE THEY WILL.

All relationships can face problems.
Those that appear to be different from
expected can have particular difficulties.
Gary's grandma is worried because
Archie is African American, and she
thinks grandpa will not approve.
Prejudice makes some people believe
that people from different races or very
different backgrounds should not form
intimate adult relationships. But it is only
the adults within any relationship who
can decide what is right for them.

Rob and Julie have just been out on their first date.
When you start going out with someone, you will want to
make a good impression. Wanting someone to like you
and not being sure how they feel can make
you very nervous and awkward. You may
not know how to behave or what to say.
You may even behave in a way you
normally wouldn't, in order to gain
approval. It is more helpful to try to
relax and just be yourself.

**Sometimes our relationship with another
person changes for reasons outside
our control.**
Gary's mom and dad no longer live
together. This means that Gary does not see
his father as much as he would like, and
misses him. Some people spend a great
deal of time wishing situations were
different. In the end, we all sometimes have
to accept that we can't have everything as
we would like. Learning to deal with our
feelings when this happens is not easy.

LOVE

LOVE IS A COMPLICATED EMOTION. NOBODY HAS EVER REALLY UNDERSTOOD WHAT LOVE IS – YET IT PLAYS A HUGE PART IN MOST PEOPLE'S LIVES.

We use the word love in all kinds of ways. We might say that we love someone's clothes, or a T.V. program. This is obviously not the same as saying that we love a member of our family, or a special friend.

Feeling love for somebody means that we care about their well-being. Strength of feeling can't be easily measured. You will feel more strongly for some people than others. Sometimes people say that they love somebody, when what they actually feel is infatuation. This is similar to a crush, but can be very intense. It can make you forget about everything and everyone else. Similarly, we can confuse loving somebody with feeling dependent on them.

If you love someone you want the best for them.

▷ Rob had been seeing Julie for a month. One afternoon he was waiting for her outside the movie theater when the gang came along.

WE HARDLY SEE YOU ANYMORE.

YOU'RE NOT GOING TO SEE THAT GIRL AGAIN, ARE YOU? YOU HAVEN'T BEEN THE SAME SINCE YOU MET THAT GIRL.

YOU STARTED "THE ADVENTURERS." IT'S NOT THE SAME WITHOUT YOU.

HE'S LET US DOWN. HE DOESN'T WANT TO KNOW US NOW THAT HE HAS A PRECIOUS GIRLFRIEND.

WE ALL KNOW WHAT THEY'LL BE UP TO IN THE BACK ROW.

ARE YOU GOING TO KISS HER THEN, ROB?

I THINK YOUR FRIENDS ARE REALLY RUDE.

HE'D BETTER NOT TRY ANYTHING.

▷ Later Rob told his dad about his feelings for Julie.

I USED TO FEEL LIKE THAT ALL THE TIME AT 13! YOU'LL GET OVER IT.

▷ They settled down to watch the movie. Rob put his arm around Julie.

I THINK I'M IN LOVE WITH HER, DAD.

Why do you think Rob's dad hasn't taken him seriously?

Rob and Julie have been to see a romantic movie. Sometimes it is easy to confuse love with romance.

Love is more than candlelit dinners and bunches of flowers. It is a commitment to another person. It means being prepared to share bad times as well as enjoying good ones, and being able to offer support to one another when problems arise.

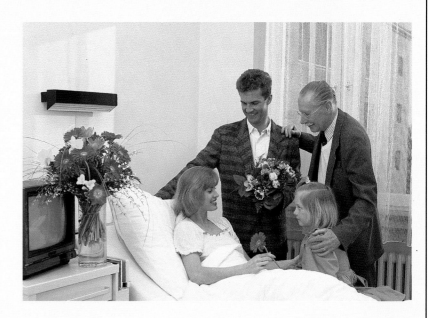

Rob feels that he is in love with Julie. However, this is his first close relationship of this kind.

Most people as they grow up will form more than one strong attachment to another person. On the other hand, although we may feel under pressure to have a boyfriend or girlfriend, there is nothing wrong with not having one. There is no rule to say that this should happen at any particular time.

Sex is an important part of many intimate grown-up relationships.

Rob's friends are making suggestive comments. Julie knows, however, that she is too young for that kind of relationship, both legally and emotionally. People's attitudes toward sex vary. Most people agree that the decision to have sex for the first time is a big step. It is vital that both people are mature enough, physically and mentally. It is not something that should be rushed into. Nobody should ever be forced into doing anything they are not happy about.

WHEN RELATIONSHIPS GO WRONG

RELATIONSHIPS DO NOT ALWAYS WORK OUT THE WAY WE WOULD LIKE. SOMETIMES THEY HAVE TO END, WHETHER WE WANT THEM TO OR NOT.

Relationships break up for many reasons. The feelings of loss and grief that we have can be very hard to face.

Problems usually arise in a relationship because one person grows to feel differently about the other. One of the reasons for this may be jealousy, or because one person has started to be possessive toward their partner. Feelings change, and sometimes people realize that their feelings about someone are not as strong as they thought they were. One partner may meet someone else they are strongly attracted to. In some cases, they may end one relationship to form another.

A lack of communication can lead to problems. If friends move away it can be difficult to keep the relationship going from a distance. Some relationships reach a natural end. If both partners realize that they are no longer committed to the relationship, they may end it in the hope of avoiding further pain or arguments.

People who are experiencing problems within a relationship sometimes seek help from a counselor.

▽ Brenda was worried about Gary.

HE'S BEEN SO MOODY LATELY. I DON'T SEEM TO BE ABLE TO GET THROUGH TO HIM.

I THINK WE BOTH KNOW THE REASON. WHY DON'T WE TAKE HIM OUT FOR A PIZZA TO CHEER HIM UP?

▽ But Gary refused to go out with them.

WHY IS HE ALWAYS TRYING TO GET ME TO LIKE HIM? HE JUST WANTS TO TAKE DAD'S PLACE.

▽ The next day Rob arranged to meet Gary.

I LIKE JULIE A LOT BUT SHE JUST WANTS TO BE FRIENDS. SHE DOESN'T WANT TO GO OUT WITH ME ANYMORE.

HE MIGHT FOOL MOM BUT HE'S NOT FOOLING ME.

SHE TOLD ME. GRANDMA SAYS YOU'RE BOTH TOO YOUNG TO GET SERIOUS ANYWAY.

MY DAD SAID THE SAME THING. BUT I KNOW I'M GOING TO FEEL JEALOUS IF SHE GOES OUT WITH SOMEONE ELSE.

LIKE RICHARD FELT JEALOUS WHEN WE BECAME FRIENDS. WHY DON'T WE GO AND SEE HIM?

▷ The three of them called a truce. They decided to go bowling.

I USED TO GO A LOT WITH MY DAD.

HEY, WHERE DID YOU LEARN TO BOWL LIKE THAT?

Is Julie's grandma right about her being too young?

Jealousy is a very intense emotion.
Richard and Gary have both felt jealous. Although everyone feels jealous at some time or other, it is not a constructive feeling. Jealousy can make you distrust those who are closest to you. You may find yourself behaving in ways you would not otherwise find acceptable. In the end jealousy only hurts everyone, including yourself.

As Rob has found out, Julie doesn't feel the same way about him as he does about her.
Relationships don't always run smoothly. Like Rob, you can care a great deal about someone, and not have your affection returned. If you like somebody and want to be close to them, it may be very hard to understand why their feelings are not as strong as yours. The reasons are not always easy to accept. Like Julie, some people may not want to get too involved in one relationship. They may prefer to be free to enjoy themselves with friends. It is important to be honest with yourself and the other person about how you feel.

Rob and Richard have realized that their friendship is too important to let their differences come between them.
Sometimes relationships break up because people cannot admit they are wrong.
Or they may feel it is up to the other person to apologize or make the first move. This sort of situation is not helpful. It is much better to swallow your pride and talk about your feelings honestly.

MAKING RELATIONSHIPS WORK

NO TWO RELATIONSHIPS ARE ALIKE. NOBODY CAN GUARANTEE HOW EACH WILL TURN OUT.

There are, however, several factors that most people agree contribute to a successful relationship.
Being able to talk about feelings and ideas, and really listening to the other person are essential. People in long-term relationships often talk about the importance of working together through any problems that come up. This is better than ignoring difficulties, and hoping that they will go away. It is necessary to be able to forgive others, and not bear grudges. In any relationship we have to know when to step back and allow others time and space to sort out their feelings. If someone feels restricted by another person, they may grow to resent the relationship.

If we work at relationships, they can be a lot of fun.

▷ Three weeks later it was Brenda's birthday. She and Archie were on their way to a party.

GARY SEEMS HAPPIER THESE DAYS. I'M BEGINNING TO THINK HE MIGHT EVEN BE GETTING USED TO ME.

I THINK SO. JULIE'S CALMED DOWN LATELY, TOO. SHE SEEMS TO HAVE HER HEAD SCREWED ON AS FAR AS BOYS ARE CONCERNED.

▽ Brenda told her mom how happy she was feeling.

I ENJOY BEING WITH ARCHIE. I FIND HIM EASY TO TALK TO.

IT'S SO IMPORTANT TO BE ABLE TO TALK ABOUT YOUR FEELINGS. I THINK GARY'S BEGUN TO UNDERSTAND THAT, TOO.

▽ Brenda got Gary up to dance. She knew it was at times like this that he especially missed his dad.

I'M SORRY I WAS HORRIBLE TO ARCHIE. HE'S REALLY NICE. BUT IT'S NOT THE SAME.

RELATIONSHIPS TAKE TIME, GARY. SOMETIMES PEOPLE TRY TOO HARD. YOU HAVE TO BE CERTAIN OF YOUR OWN FEELINGS.

YOUR DAD AND I BROKE UP, BUT HE'LL ALWAYS BE YOUR DAD. WHATEVER HAPPENS WITH ARCHIE AND ME, NOTHING CAN EVER CHANGE THAT.

▽ Gary knew that his mom was right.

TO BRENDA. HAPPY BIRTHDAY!

HAPPY BIRTHDAY!

Good relationships can take time to develop.
Brenda knows that she cannot tell yet whether she and Archie will continue to see each other. She is prepared to wait and find out what happens. She knows that rushing into a relationship is not wise, and expecting too much too quickly can often lead to problems.

Both Brenda and her mom understand how important it is to be able to communicate in a relationship.
Trust and honesty are vital if a close relationship is going to succeed. Being open about your feelings allows the other person to get to know you well, and lets you share your experiences. Keeping secrets or not being able to talk to each other can cause problems. Many people who enjoy successful relationships say it is important to allow people to be themselves. They do not believe in trying to change the other person.

Relationships are not fixed. They change over time.
We are always meeting new people, or finding out new things about those we already know. People in relationships should not be seen as possessions. We all need space to express ourselves. It would be boring if everything and everybody stayed the same. People are always developing new interests and going in different directions. This is what makes relationships exciting.

WHAT CAN WE DO?

HAVING READ THIS BOOK, YOU WILL UNDERSTAND MORE ABOUT HOW DIFFERENT KINDS OF RELATIONSHIPS CAN AFFECT YOU.

You will already be familiar with many of these relationships. Others you will probably experience at some time in your life. When you form a relationship with another person, you are sharing part of yourself with that person. It is therefore essential to know yourself well, and to like yourself. We cannot expect others to like us if we don't like ourselves. All relationships have their ups and downs. They need work from all involved if they are to be successful. People who truly care about each other don't just give up at the first sign of problems.

Kids' Fund
P.O. Box 829
Planetarium Station
New York, NY 10024
212-580-8228

Family Services America
11700 W. Lake Park Drive
Milwaukee, WT 53224
800-221-2681

Committee For Children
2203 Airport Way S.
Suite 500
Seattle, WA 98134-2027
800-634-4449

ADULTS ARE SOMETIMES NOT AWARE HOW MUCH INFLUENCE THEIR RELATIONSHIPS HAVE ON THEIR CHILDREN.

Growing up in an environment where adults argue, or don't seem to care about each other, can affect the way young people view relationships.
Adults and young people who have read this book together may find it helpful to share their own ideas and experiences of relationships. People who are experiencing problems with a relationship may wish to talk to somebody not directly involved. The organizations listed below will be able to provide information and support.

Stepfamily Foundation
333 West End Avenue
New York, NY 10023
800-SKY-STEP

Family Resource Coalition
20 N. Wacker Drive
Suite 1100
Chicago, IL 60606
312-338-0900

The Education Development Center
55 Chapel Street
Newton, MA 02158
800-225-4276

The National Board For Certified Counselors
3D Terrace Way
Greensboro, NC 27403
910-547-0607

The National Association of Social Workers
750 First Street NE
Suite 700
Washington, DC 20002
202-408-8600

INDEX

Photocredits

All the pictures in this book are by Roger Vlitos apart from page 4: Robert Harding Picture Library; page 14: Topham Picture Source; pages 23 top and 30: Spectrum Colour Library.